THIS BOOK
BELONGS TO